LIFE
DRAWING

**PETER STANYER &
TERRY ROSENBERG**

ARCTURUS

INTRODUCTION

The life room is a peculiar place and life drawing is a bizarre activity. A group of people crowd round and draw a – usually naked – figure who they, more often than not, do no know. They try to wrest a likeness of the model by dint of effort and skill. However, often they do not reflect on the ways in which they are doing this or to what end. Before embarking on a programme of life drawing, you need to ask yourself how and why you are doing it. Your answers to these two questions should qualify each other. How you draw is contingent on why you are drawing.

We do not dispute that life drawing is an important aspect of an art education, but if it is to be significant, it must extend into the rest of life and begin to touch upon things that matter to you. Otherwise it is an empty activity – the development of a skill with no purpose. It is necessary to point out the limitations of the life room so that you may eventually use the activity fruitfully. People bring many preconceptions to the figure. We tend to know it too well and in too many ways. We know the human body from within and without. This knowledge is essential for drawing, but if it isn't edited it can be inhibiting in both drawing and seeing. We need to find equivalents for our feelings, thoughts and observations of the figure in the ways we see and depict it.

As we draw the human figure, we reveal and we hide ourselves, and it. We need to be aware of what it is we need to reveal. What is the occasion and purpose of the drawing? Is it a rite of magic, or worship? A reflection of the domestic or public figure? A figure to be venerated or hated? Further, how does it speak of drawing itself?

On the opposite page is a wonderful etching by Rembrandt. Its subject is life drawing. Rembrandt depicts himself seated, drawing. Over his right shoulder a figure with quill and measuring staff watches over him. A muse? A spirit of

Etching by Rembrandt of himself drawing the model.

drawing? In front of Rembrandt is a model, modestly clutching a drape hiding part of her body. She is the subject of his drawing, the object of his gaze. The quill of the muse is exaggerated in the palm that is in the model's space. In the background, on a ledge, a bust looks down on the proceedings, distanced but involved.

The etching looks unfinished, but is it? A number of different approaches to drawing are revealed: different speeds of drawing and looking; different perceptual attitudes; different truths. The artist himself is realised through a flurry of marks (which we shall understand later in the book as gestural drawing); the muse and the model are realised more particularly in a line contour, and the bust through a progression of tone.

The idea that there is one true way of representing the figure is anathema. Human vision is complex, and a drawing cannot contain the full panoply of our perception. Drawing is something else, albeit causally linked to our perception. To draw, one needs to seek for what connects drawing to the real and to know that there is a space between 'reality' and a drawing; and that this space is the space of invention.

Within the limits of this book, we aim to open up some of the possible ways of drawing the figure. These are, for the most part, approaches used in the Western tradition. There is much, still, that remains outside the book's domain, but we hope that it will lay the groundwork for future explorations.

CHAPTER 1

HAND, EYE AND MIND

Before you start to draw, you will need to organise yourself, your equipment and the model. It is important that you arrange the best possible situation in which to draw. Position yourself so that you can see the whole figure. Place your drawing paper on a firm board and fix it with clips, masking tape or pins. Then position the board so that the look from the figure to the drawing involves just a slight turn of the head. Do not position the board in front of the figure or you will have to move to see round it.

If you are using A1 paper (which is recommended for the projects), it is best to stand at an easel. If an easel is not available you can make do, but try to make sure that you stand far enough away from the drawing while you work that you can see all or the greater part of it in one view. If not, keep moving back from the drawing to look at it from a distance. If possible, organise your position so that the hand you draw with is the one furthest from the model. Your drawing arm will not then obstruct your view. See that the paper is at a good height; your eye line should be about one-third of the way down from the top of the paper. This will avoid the distortion, called error of parallax, that occurs when you look at a sheet of paper at an acute angle.

PRELIMINARY DRAWING
One 20-minute drawing
Materials: *A1 cartridge paper, pencil or charcoal*

When you are ready, start on an untutored drawing from the model. Imagine you are in a class situation and draw continuously for 20 minutes. Do not exceed the time allotted and do not renege on the drawing. When the 20 minutes are up, consider the following questions:
What were you trying to convey in the drawing?
What did you convey?
What eluded you?

Were there other ways in which you could have captured it?
How were you drawing – in terms both of looking at the model and making the drawing?
What would you have done differently if the drawing time were longer – 6 hours, say?
What would you have done in 5 minutes?
Would you take more care over the 6-hour drawing? In what way?
Would you make it more accurate? If so, what does that mean and why is it desirable? And how could it be achieved?

A drawing is a product of the time in which it is done, and its speed of production is part of its meaning, so the way you look and draw needs to be appropriate to the time you have. Keep the drawing you have done as a comparison for what comes later.

The projects in this chapter require you to place yourself in a number of unorthodox situations in your confrontation with both the model and your drawings, in an attempt to encourage you to reflect on the mechanics and mechanisms of drawing – sense and motor-sense, looking and the process of looking, pencil and paper. The projects will also help you to see drawing as an attempt to understand what it means to draw in terms of the optical, mental and physical apparatus involved. It would be churlish not to admit that the projects are also an attempt to break down, or at least question, preconceptions and ingrained habits that you may have about drawing.

At the same time, these exercises are intended to be fun, and should be approached in that spirit because it is through lighthearted disruptions of our normal methods of drawing that we can open up new questions and opportunities. Please try to shed any restricting expectations, such as trying to match the look of another drawing. Drawing is a creative process; it is not the matching of something that already exists. To try to do so is affected and mannered and has no place in 'real' drawing. Having said that, during the process of drawing you will experience times when what you have in the drawing does not accord with what you feel you should have. This is inherent in the creative act. Stick with it because it is essential to progress the drawing beyond these points. You will not know what is possible in a drawing unless you have a determination to push it beyond its sticky moments.

THE GESTURE

A gesture is an action that has significance – the gift of a bunch of flowers, or the movement of a pencil on a sheet of paper. In drawing, gesture is the action of the hand and drawing tool as they follow the movement of the eye while it scans the figure.

The activity of looking is selective and goal-directed: the eye darts over the field of vision, seeking and selecting pertinent features in the field and dovetailing these with the mind's means of making sense of them. The gestural drawing is one that follows the eye's search for meaning; it should be a quick search, seeing and placing the whole figure almost at once.

PROJECT 1
GESTURE DRAWINGS

Three 5-minute drawings
Materials: *A1 cartridge/newsprint paper, pencil*
Pose the model and draw with speed and pressure. Take a full 5 minutes over each drawing.

Use your A1 sheet of paper in landscape format so that you can get all three drawings on one sheet. Ask the model to take a different pose for each drawing, and try to get all or most of the figure on the page. Draw at a reasonable scale in relation to the size of the paper because fear for and of a drawing results in a reduction in scale and timid marks on the paper.

You need to approach this with confidence. After all, you are only risking the cost of a sheet of paper. Regard your hand as connected to your eye; do not fix your sight or pencil on detail, but work from the general to the specific.

Let your pencil work through the drawing with a cursive line, swinging from top to bottom and side to side until the figure is drawn out.

It is obvious from the illustrations that there is no recourse to outline. At times, when students try this type of drawing, they declare that they cannot see the lines they are drawing. That is the case with any type of drawing. This confusion arises from a tendency to confuse the drawing with the real world. The lines you are drawing should relate to the way in which you

*Far left and
this page:
Gesture drawings*

are looking. They should
be infused with seeing,
following the eye as it roves
across the figure. In effect,
this type of drawing is a
scribble, but it is not an
affectation or imposition. It
relates directly to seeing.

PROJECT 2
GESTURAL DRAWINGS

One 3-minute drawing, one 1-minute drawing and one 5-minute drawing
Materials: *A1 cartridge/newsprint paper, pencil*

Do another three drawings, taking different lengths of time over each. The different times allocated for the three poses demonstrate the stages in seeing and depicting more obviously. It is important that the 1-minute and 5-minute drawings both capture the whole figure. Again, in these drawings you should move from the whole to the particular.

PROJECT 3
HAND-EYE CO-ORDINATION

Two 5-minute gestural drawings
Materials: *A1 cartridge/newsprint paper, pencil*
The approach in this project starts to break down any intentions that you might have about how you want the drawing to turn out.

In these two drawings your eyes should be on the model continuously while you work. All the time that your pencil is moving, you should be looking at the model. Although this is difficult, try not to cheat. You can look at your drawing a couple of times, but not while your pencil is on the paper.

What we are attending to here is hand-eye co-ordination. When playing tennis, if you are to do it well, you watch and address the ball. You do not watch the racquet on its path to the ball. You know that your arm will act in accordance with information from the eye and instructions from the brain. The same type of sense is highly developed in most artists.

PROJECT 4

GESTURAL DRAWING — UNFAVOURED HAND

Two 5-minute drawings
Materials: *A1 cartridge/newsprint paper, pencil*

The movements of your favoured hand are rooted in habit — from writing, work, or other kinds of drawing — whereas the unfavoured hand will open up the creative, less predetermined side of drawing.

The drawings in this project are to be done with your unfavoured hand. If you are left-handed, use your right hand, and if right-handed use your left hand. The lines made in these drawings will have an expressive quality lacking in drawings made with the favoured hand, and this approach will help to develop an expressiveness that can only emerge when your intentioning faculties are suspended.

THE CONTINUOUS LINE

The continuous line is much as it sounds. The drawing is done continuously and at a constant speed without lifting the hand from the paper. Progress the drawing rhythmically, continuously comparing the elements and features of the figure and setting to each other. The line is produced more slowly than in a gestural drawing. Rather than being a scribble, the drawing looks as if it has been done with a length of wire. (You could consider realising some of your completed continuous-line drawings in wire.)

PROJECT 5
CONTINUOUS-LINE DRAWING

Three 5-minute drawings
Materials: *A1 cartridge/newsprint paper, pencil, conté or charcoal pencil*

Place your pencil on the paper and convince yourself that it is a particular point on the model. Move your eye and hand at a steady rate round the model, locating the features without looking at the drawing. You will have to move over areas without edges in your search, comparing and locating points in relation to each other as you go. The rough proportions of the figure will become established in this search.

PROJECT 6
HOLDING THE DRAWING IMPLEMENT

Three 5-minute drawings
Materials: *A1 cartridge/newsprint paper, pencil, charcoal, felt-tip pen or biro*

The different movements of our bodies create different marks on paper, so we need to question further the actions involved in making a drawing. We can generate marks through movements of the fingers, or from the wrist, elbow or shoulder, or even the whole body. Try all approaches, and you will find that each demands that you draw on a different scale and brings about a different type of expressiveness. The following exercises explore the different ways in which a drawing tool can be held and moved.

Hold the drawing implement like a dagger being used in a crime of passion: in the palm of the hand with your fingers wrapped around it and the drawing point by your little finger. Draw for 5 minutes with a continuous line.

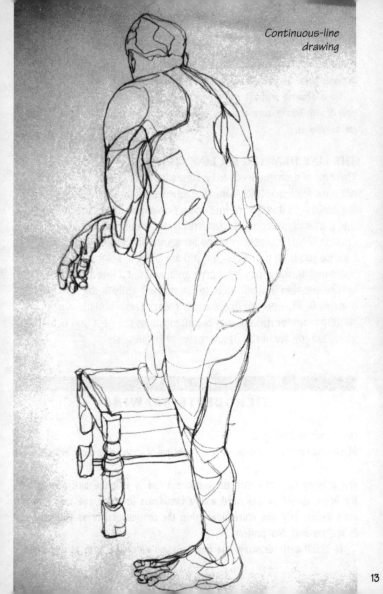

Continuous-line
drawing

Hold the pencil between thumb and first finger as far away from the drawing point as possible. Draw for 5 minutes.

Do a drawing without using your hands — try holding the implement in your mouth (make sure you are not using charcoal!) or foot. Again, draw for 5 minutes.

THE LINE DRAWING OR LINE CONTOUR

This type of drawing needs to be done with a confident, incisive line. Do not use a feathered line — one that moves back on itself before proceeding again — as this type of line doesn't overcome any of the problems that it tries to overcome. It just reflects its own uncertainty. A line drawing requires confidence and arrogance on the part of the artist because you have to believe that you are going to get it right (your untutored drawing may have been an attempt at a line drawing).

The question that you need to ask yourself while doing this type of drawing is: where is the line actually going? The silhouette is a good starting point for this enquiry because it shows the edge that is made where the surface of the figure curves away out of sight.

PROJECT 7

SILHOUETTE DRAWING

One 10-minute drawing
Materials: *A1 cartridge/newsprint paper, pencil, charcoal or conté, eraser*

This drawing has links with the continuous line in that the outside edges of the figure should be described with a continuous line, but one that is made more deliberately and more slowly than the continuous line as you used it in the previous two projects.

In a silhouette drawing, the line must not enter the form at any point, but you should draw the spaces between, for example, arm and body through which you can see the background — the negative spaces. You can use an eraser to correct mistakes.

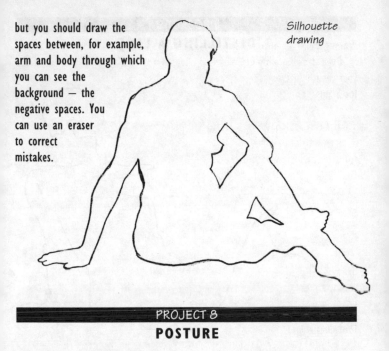

Silhouette drawing

PROJECT 8
POSTURE

Three 3-minute drawings
Materials: *A1 cartridge/newsprint paper, pencil, charcoal or conté, eraser*
Lines can be used to capture the model's posture.

Posture lines have little to do with the silhouette, but instead record the way the pose is held, describing and accenting the angles made by and between different parts of the body: for example, the angles across the shoulders, down the middle of the body, across the top part of the body, along the limbs, across the brow and down the middle of the face. The result is a drawing that looks a little like a stick figure.

PROJECT 9
DISTILLING A LINE

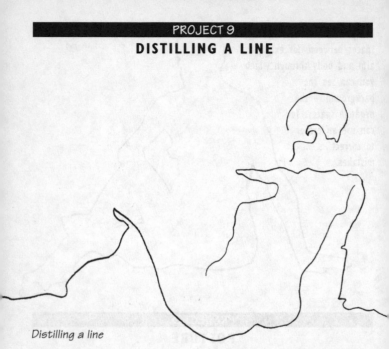

Distilling a line

Three 3-minute drawings
Materials: A1 cartridge/newsprint paper, pencil, charcoal or conté, eraser
To distil the pose to its essential lines, find one line to follow that describes the pose as fully as possible.

The line can move from the silhouette through the posture. This exercise is linked to the continuous-line drawing in that it runs from one edge to another across the form, using an opportune feature to do so. Then add two more lines to the first to give a clearer indication of the whole pose. The lines should have confidence and dynamism.

PROJECT 10

THE LINE OR LINE-CONTOUR DRAWING

Three 20-minute drawings
Materials: *A1 paper, pencil or pen*
Line can be used to describe the edge of a form, working with the line on the other side to encompass the whole form.

The silhouette drawing works if the lines around the figure continue across the masses they are describing so as to cup them. If a mime artist were to act out catching a ball, his two hands would work together to hold it. They would cup the ball, each hand forming a convex arc around the sphere of the ball. In a similar way, the line drawing seeks to describe the volume of the trunk, head and limbs by using the line and its inflection (the line on the other side of the form) to capture the form. However, it is a little

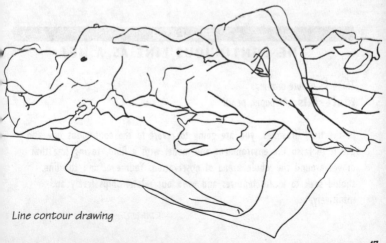

Line contour drawing

Body-builders seek to build their muscles up so that they are dramatically 'cut' — the muscles are clearly defined through the skin. In using a line to describe a contour, you are bringing the line into the form to seek the edges of the volume of muscle or fat — in other words, using the 'cut' of the form to describe how one volume sits in front of another. Make sure that the illusion of overlap works the right way round to show which volume sits in front of which.

more complex than that. The figure is not a puppet; the limbs, body and head are not composed of simple, standard volumes (see 'Building Blocks'). Muscle, fat and bone also need to be described. The drawing (previous page) shows how the line can break away from the silhouette and enter the form to seek the internal volumes. Using a line in this way, you can explore how one form sits in front of another.

Do three line-contour drawings with pencil or pen, spending 20 minutes on each one.

PROJECT 11
THE CONTINUOUS LINE AS A NET

Three 15-minute drawings
Materials: A1 paper, pencil

In the final drawings, you are going to revert to the continuous line and use it to lasso the environment and model with a fluid, roving line that moves around the whole arena of observation. Your eye, and the line, should seek to locate features and work out relationships freely and intuitively.

Right: Continuous line as a net

CHAPTER 2

THROUGH THE WINDOW

In trying to draw the human figure, students often declare that the major problem lies in getting the proportions right. In our attempts to understand the visual world, we note and organise categories of similarity and difference, seeking connections and relationships in the subjects we are looking at, apportioning relevance and meaning. So, in a drawing, what are these proportions that elude us and what methods are there for bringing them about?

In the projects in the previous chapter you were encouraged to draw with freedom, unencumbered by strict methods of measurement and mapping. Yet you were measuring, in the sense that your mind directed your eye to seek and organise the relationships between features and elements in the figure, and you sought to find equivalents for that search with your pencil on the paper. And as you become more practised and experienced, you will be able to assess proportions more easily in this fluid way.

There is notional agreement on what is proportional. We know proportion to be a scale of comparison. But what is the scale against which we are calibrating the constituents in a drawing? Many different scales are used in different types of art.

In the art of Ancient Egypt, the size of a figure was relative to his or her position in society. The pharoahs were drawn larger than their soldiers, noblemen larger than their slaves. Children's drawings exhibit another type of scale of importance. For the child, the face carries more information than the body. It is where identity and moods – the features of social intercourse that are most important to the child – are located. In a child's drawing, therefore, the face is given emphasis, and the body is diminished in size. Architects and designers may scale down actual sizes in their drawings to provide clearer instructions. Different cultures use different scales for the objects and elements in the world contingent on their viewpoint, the story and the purpose of the drawing. All of these are valid and have specific uses in visual communication.

What we have unwittingly conformed to in the drawings in the previous chapter, and consciously buy into when we talk of correct proportion and measurement, is a system of seeing and depicting known as linear or 'peephole ' perspective, which was evolved as a theory by the Renaissance painter and architect Leon Battista Alberti (1404-72), and immediately taken up by other Renaissance artists, such as Filippo Brunelleschi (1377-1446). Linear perspective is a system for organising the geometrical relationships of the three-dimensional world on a two-dimensional surface. Alberti equates the picture plane and the drawing surface with a window where a one-eyed, motionless artist mechanically observes and maps the petrified scene on the far side of the window onto the plane of the window – the picture plane.

Leonardo da Vinci (1452-1519) in his notebooks describes a procedure for drawing that illustrates Alberti's theory:

'Have a piece of glass as large as a half sheet of royal folio paper and set this firmly in front of your eyes, that is between your eye and the thing you want to draw; then place yourself at a distance of 2/3 of a braccio [a bracchio = approximately 1m/1 yd] from the glass, fixing your head with a machine in such a way that you cannot move at all. Then shut or cover one eye and with a brush or drawing chalk draw upon the glass that which you see beyond it.'

Put more simply, hold up a sheet of glass between you and the scene you wish to draw. Cover one eye and find a way to fix the relationship between your eye, the sheet of glass and the scene by lining up specific points in the subject and the background. Then, keeping absolutely still, intercept the visual rays projected from the objects of your gaze onto the retina at the point where they pass through the sheet of glass. In other words, diligently trace what lies beyond the window.

If this is followed assiduously, there shouldn't be a problem in getting different features in proportion to one another. All that is needed is some kind of mechanism for holding all the relationships constant. In Leonardo's notebook there is a sketch of apparatus to help in this kind of drawing. In Albrecht Durer's treatise, *On Measurement and Proportion* (1525), four drawing machines are illustrated. These were evolved to determine and fix relationships between the eye, the window and the scene in a systematic way in order to locate and plot the lines projected from the scene to the eye on the sheet of glass.

During most of our drawing we do not have the luxury of a sheet of glass or other transparent surface onto which to trace the world; nor do we have an apparatus to hold all the relationships as fixed and allow us to plot them (although a rudimentary machine can be constructed). We therefore need to imagine Alberti's window lying between us and the scene and find strategies and procedures for transferring what we see at this imagined window onto our opaque and unaligned sheet of paper. The three projects that follow describe three different procedures for analysing the information at Alberti's window and transferring it onto the drawing support. They require a great deal of concentration and assiduous method.

The drawings in the previous chapter employed strategies to disrupt the part of our seeing that links itself to spoken and written language (controlled by the left hemisphere of the brain) and to tap into the less rational, more intuitive part of the brain (the right hemisphere). That is, they were designed to remove from your endeavours a literal way of seeing. Ultimately, however, drawing should not be limited by confining our thinking to one hemisphere or the other. It relies on both the intuitive and rational methods of approach. Some students have difficulties with the following exercises because they find the way of seeing and thinking that is demanded too methodical and too weighted in the left hemisphere of the brain. However, although you may never want to set about a drawing in such a systematic way again, the methods of determining proportion and position will nevertheless help in future drawings, and you can adapt the methods put forward here to suit your own ends.

METHODS OF ANALYSIS

In the following exercises you are trying to extract the information observed at Alberti's window and transfer it onto the drawing paper. To do this, you need to take measurements and directions from the window. The straight line is the most appropriate means of fixing the relationship between two points because it is constant in both trajectory and length.

The best way to determine the angle between two points is to place a straight-edged instrument (a pencil or ruler will do) flat on the imagined plane of Alberti's window. Make sure it is flat on the imagined plane, not tilted into it in any way. Swing the straight-edge between the two points to be assessed and then transfer the angled instrument to your picture. Hold the straight-edge against the paper and draw the angle in the appropriate position. You can also find the angle by assessing it against an imaginary horizontal or vertical line.

To determine the length and position of elements in a picture, a predetermined unit of measurement is needed that can be used to read off measurements in the correct scale at the 'window' and transfer them to the drawing. There are three ways in which this can be done. The window-frame itself can be used as a measuring device. The axes of measurement can be applied to the subject at the window and consequently to the drawing. Or the features of the figure and scene can be used as units of measurement.

PROJECT 1

USING A WINDOW-MOUNT AS A MEASURING DEVICE

One 3-hour drawing
Materials: *A1 cartridge paper, charcoal*
This exercise employs a rough piece of drawing apparatus to measure the angles in the model.

MAKING A WINDOW-MOUNT

Take a piece of card or stiff paper and cut a rectangle out of the centre in the same proportions as your drawing paper.

Divide the inner edges of the rectangle into quarters and mark these divisions at the edge of the window with a pencil. If you wish, you could run a piece of thread between the appropriate divisions to set up a gridded window-mount. The window should not be too large or too small – 25cm (10 in) along the longest side is about right.

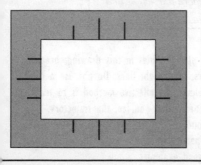

Compose the model, yourself and your easel or drawing rest and fix your position in relation to the model's. Next, find your composition using the window-mount. Move the window-mount to left and right, and backwards and forwards, until you have found the scene you wish to draw. Fix the window-mount in relation to yourself. Some students fix the frame to the drawing board. If this isn't appropriate, hold the mount in your hand and make a mental note of the distance and position of your hand in relation to your eye. Close one eye and see how features in the scene align with the markings on the window-mount so that you can return the mount to the same position should you move. As your hand will tire, this is more than likely.

Lightly mark the divisions of the window onto your drawing surface. Using one eye to measure, proceed to draw by finding the place where a feature starts at the edge of the mount (e.g., the floor/wall line, a tabletop or the figure itself). Draw in the angle (Step 1). Try to produce a silhouette through the analysis of vectors while using the frame to find the positions of different features (Step 2). Work through the whole figure and its setting in the same way, determining direction and angle from the sides of the frame (Step 3).

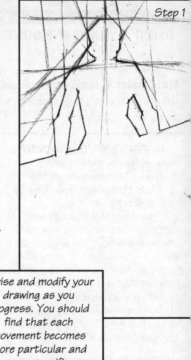

Step 1

Revise and modify your drawing as you progress. You should find that each movement becomes more particular and more specific.

Remember that you are trying to draw your mode of analysing the subject in front of you, not the subject itself. There should only be straight lines in this drawing; break down curves into a series of vectors, or straight lines. Do not use a ruler for these lines, but draw them freehand. An effective method is to track the line with a light, repeated movement so that you feel the trajectory, extending the vector beyond the contour into the space, setting up a web of measurement that captures the particulars of the view. The drawings of Alberto Giacometti (1901-66) are good examples.

Measuring with a
window-mount

It is a good idea to mark
around the model, your
feet and the feet of the
easel or rest with chalk
or charcoal in order to fix
the relationships between
the three. Then, when you
or the model take a
break, you can both easily
return to the same
position.

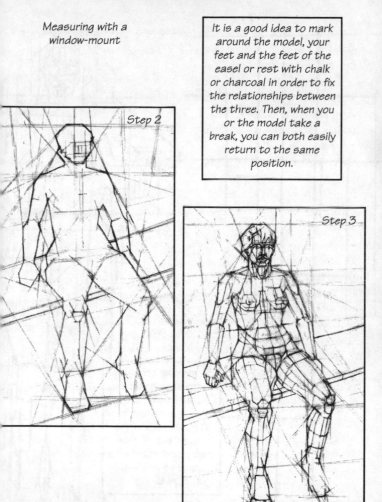

Step 2

Step 3

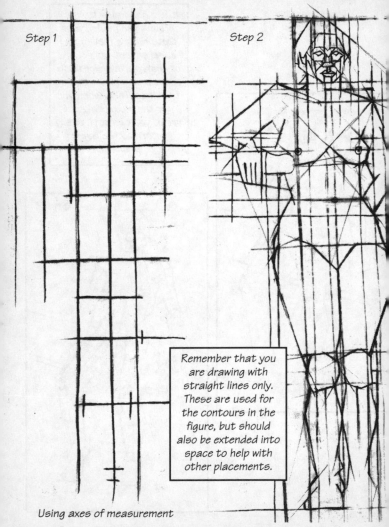

Step 1

Step 2

Remember that you
are drawing with
straight lines only.
These are used for
the contours in the
figure, but should
also be extended into
space to help with
other placements.

Using axes of measurement

AXES OF MEASUREMENT

One 3-hour drawing
Materials: *A1 cartridge paper, pencil, conté or charcoal pencil*
This project dispenses with the frame as a measuring instrument. Instead, horizontal and vertical axes are going to be established within the picture, against which the subject can be measured.

Draw a vertical line on the sheet of paper at the place where you wish to place the figure. Decide the scale at which you want to draw, and mark where you want the top and bottom of the figure to fall on the vertical line. At the top point of the figure draw a horizontal line.

Hold your pencil (or other straight-edged instrument) up to the model. Hold it at arm's length as this fixes absolutely its distance from your eye. Make the top of the pencil coincide with the top of the model's head. Move your thumb down to mark the bottom of the chin. Other elements of the figure can be used, but the head is the preferred unit for measuring. See how many of these units — heads — fit into the full length of the figure. Divide the vertical line on your paper into the same number of units. The head size on the pencil need not be the same as the head in the drawing. Just remember that you are fixing the scale of the drawing against the head so that other elements can be determined as so many heads or as fractions of the head. Mark off a number of 'head' units on the horizontal axis (Step 1).

Develop the drawing using the horizontal and vertical axes drawn on the paper, extending other horizontal and vertical lines from these to determine the scale of features in the composition. Place the larger components first, using postural analysis (see 'Hand, Eye and Mind', Project 8) to determine the angles and scale of the pose (Step 2). Continue until the drawing is complete.

PROJECT 3
FEATURES AS MEASURING UNITS

One 3-hour drawing
Materials: *A3 cartridge paper, HB pencil*
In this drawing you will tackle a portrait. This is probably the most difficult subject when you are trying not to be too literal. Keep to the method described, however, and it should turn out all right.

You are going to evolve this drawing by relating the features in the drawing one to another. It is easier, and perhaps better, to work from the whole head shape (called the blank) to the features, but you can proceed

> *Consider the quality of line that you are using and aim to develop a feeling of precision in its movement.*

from feature to feature, although the room for error is greater with this

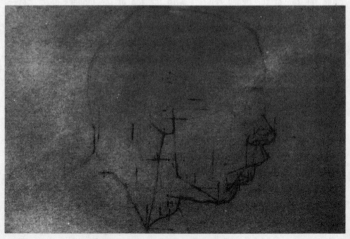

Features used as measuring units

method. Yet again, you need to set one unit as a constant for measurement. This can be anything — for example, the length of the nose or the distance from forehead to chin. Mark the unit on the page at the scale you want for the drawing. Assess and mark on the paper the points at the limits of features and movements. Draw in the contour as you proceed. It need not be drawn with a straight line in this drawing. Keep your drawing fluid through the process, allowing yourself to review and revise throughout.

FORESHORTENING

Foreshortening has been the bugbear of a great number of students of drawing. It is a particular feature of peephole perspective. It occurs when the figure, or part of the figure, is not on a parallel plane to the picture; i.e., it lies back in the illusory space. Our normal expectations of the proportions of the body will be quite alarmingly confounded by the projections of the proportions of the body onto the picture plane. Near elements will seem exaggeratedly large, further elements incredibly small. Trust your measurement and method; hold your disbelief in check, and when you

Foreshortened figure

produce the whole context, the drawing will be accurately foreshortened.

The first known drawing of a figure foreshortened appears in a panel of Paolo Uccello's *Battle of San Romano* (1450s) in the National Gallery, London. It is a marvellous if somewhat reduced figure.

CHAPTER 3

A PROGRESSION OF TONE

I t is in light and through light that we see. Consequently, drawing is a product of light, and all marks on paper are read in and by light. When we deposit a ribbon of pigment on a support, what we read is the contrast in lightness and darkness between the pigment and the support. Even the inscribed or etched line is picked out through light. A blind person may feel the contour of the engraved or raised line, but the line is envisioned in light.

In drawing, 'tone' (sometimes called 'value') is an index of light. Lines, marks, rubbings, smears, can be made with drawing materials of different tonal values to create different gradations of light or dark. You can also achieve this gradation using one drawing medium, by increasing and decreasing the pressure you apply as you draw, thus leaving varying amounts of pigment on the drawing surface. On many occasions in the life room, and indeed in other drawing situations, students will 'add tone' to their drawings by placing a series of smudges on the figure in the hope of making it look more 'real'. The student may be trying to describe the texture or the anatomy of the figure, but in many cases all that they achieve is a dirtying of the picture because the marks they have made do not equate with the optical, intellectual or expressive aspects of looking. As a result, the student is often frustrated by the effect that they have created.

The different ways in which tone can be used need to be addressed in order to avoid this confusion. Let us consider four distinct applications: outline, modelling, colour and cast shadows.

THE OUTLINE

The outline, as we have already witnessed in the silhouette (see 'Hand Eye and Mind', Project 7), declares the limits of the volumes of the figure when projected onto the picture plane. You need to consider the weight of the line that you use to draw the outline because you can establish different expressions and different readings of the three-dimensional world that you are depicting, depending on how you use the line.

Tone can be used to modulate the outline of a figure. In Graeco-Roman, Byzantine, medieval and folkloric art, and in the drawings of modern artists such as Pierre Auguste Renoir (1841-1919) and Aristide Maillol (1861-1944), a dark tone or value is bled into the form from the outline, creating a penumbra, or graduated shadow, around the inner edges. Artists use this technique to emphasise the volume of the forms — in other words, as an elementary type of modelling.

Shading can also be used outside the forms to qualify the space around them, creating the effect of air by emphasising the difference between form and space. A highlight can also be used inside or outside the figure to model either the forms or the space. The technical terms for the deployment of tone in this way are endotropic (if it is used inside the form) or exotropic (if it is used outside the form), shadow (if it is a darker value) or highlight (if it is a light value).

Endotropic and exotropic tone can also be used (with restraint) where different areas of the same tonal value meet, in order to distinguish the edge where the two abut. In this case, tone should be applied with a broken mark along the edge, and it should become more diffuse as it moves into the area being worked. The edge needs to be broken in order to state that it is a tonal mark and not a second outline. These shadows and highlights are not 'out there', seen in the subject. They are part of the artifice of drawing and help to emphasise particular aspects of what is observed.

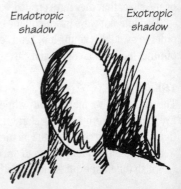

Endotropic shadow

Exotropic shadow

MODELLING

Shadow can be used to model forms. By darkening the inside edges of convex forms (endotropic shadow), you can make these edges appear to push further into the picture space, causing the lit middle area of the form to come forward. This notion of the plasticity of form, however, assumes that light is hitting the form smack in the middle, and that the edges are, therefore, in partial or full shadow.

In the drawings of Renaissance artists such as Raphael (1483-1520) and Michelangelo (1475-1564), for example, there isn't a universal light source for the whole figure. The forms of the muscles are dealt with as discrete masses, each meriting its own light source. Light is used to model each form as and when necessary; no matter where the muscle or muscle group is, it is lit centrally.

Tone pushes edge back into page

Lit middle comes forward

Tonal penumbra modelling of ovoid

COLOUR

Both the figure and its environment are coloured. Different colours carry different tonal values. In a drawing, light yellow, for example, may appear as a very light grey, and deep purple as a very dark grey. When using a monochromatic scale – one without a hue (red, yellow, blue and so on), but consisting of a range of greys from white through to black – tonality is the only aspect of colour that you can convey in a drawing. However, you can use tone as a pigment – filling in areas of a drawing to create contrasts for their aesthetic merit (drama, balance and so on) – rather than as a description of light.

CAST SHADOWS

When light from a particular source falls on an object, the surfaces of the object that face the light source will be lit and the surfaces that do not face it will be in shadow. The shadow that is produced is an echo of the object, but it is modified by its distance from the form and by the nature of the surface on which it is cast.

By taking into account and addressing the effect of light from partic-ular sources (there may be several light sources, or you may elect to address only the primary source), you can produce a progression of tone on the picture surface that duplicates the pattern of light in the scene, giving further clues to depth and form. In many instances, you need draw only the shadow produced by one strong light source to achieve a strong reading of a figure, face, object or scene.

While you are drawing the effect of directional light on a scene, it is crucial that you keep the mechanism of the eye constant; that is, you need to keep the pupils at a constant aperture (as in the 'F' stop of a camera). The pupils usually expand and contract as they move through dark and light areas of the scene, and this will confuse the tonal infor-mation for a drawing. By squinting, you can restrict the pupils to one 'setting', allowing you to make consistent judgements across the

Cast shadows

complete scene. You can then make particular comparisons for details with your eyes open.

When you are doing a drawing that rests on observations of a directional light, your main aim should be to locate and record the effect of that light; you are describing the surfaces in light and those in shadow, and portraying the shadows cast. Materials and textures affect the impression of light that we receive — the effect of light falling on fur differs from that on glass. However, in this chapter we are looking at light in relation to form and space rather than surface texture.

PROJECT 1

GESTURAL TONE

Two 30-minute drawings
Materials: A3 cartridge paper, conté pencil or fine felt-tip pen

In these drawings, first establish the figure and then set up a strong directional light in order to explore the tonal range. The drawings should be done almost lackadaisically, like a doodle. Pose the model and start to draw gesturally, swinging your drawing tool around the paper and trying to locate the whole scene at once, fluidly and easily. Aim to encapsulate the major aspects of the model in the first 5 minutes. Do not concern yourself with tone yet. Next, light the scene, positioning the light to one side so that the subject is lit dramatically. Darken the room too, if this adds to the drama. If you light the model from close to your own position, you will not see any shadow on the model and the figure will appear flattened.

Squint at the subject as you draw, which will allow you a consistent comparison between tones throughout your whole field of vision. Draw the patches of observed shadow, and use endotropic and exotropic shadow (again with the gestural spirit) to qualify the forms and space.

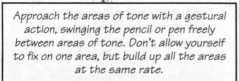

Approach the areas of tone with a gestural
action, swinging the pencil or pen freely
between areas of tone. Don't allow yourself
to fix on one area, but build up all the areas
at the same rate.

PROJECT 2

SUBTRACTIVE TONE

One 3-hour drawing
Materials: *A1 cartridge paper (white), charcoal or black pastel (not oil-based), a good, hard gum eraser and kneadable putty eraser*
In this exercise, begin by covering the paper with charcoal or pastel, and then draw into this with an eraser to record the lighter areas.

Completely blacken your drawing paper with your drawing material. Rub it lightly with newsprint to create an even tone. Draw with your hard eraser, using vectors of analysis (see 'Through the Window', Project 1) to place the figure and environment lightly and loosely. Think about the composition at this stage as well. It should take you about 15 minutes to map the figure.

Treat the figure and surroundings with equal importance. This kind of drawing only works if the whole view is integrated.
Consider the whole scene as a patchwork of the three tonal possibilities. Tone is your subject here; not model, nor table, nor floor, only tone. Try to forget everything that you know about what is in front of you.

Illuminate the figure with a strong directional light, positioning the light source so that it creates interesting conditions. You could use underlighting or some other unusual type.

If the room is very dark and the light source strong, you will have a dramatic and marked contrast, known as *chiaroscuro* (from the Italian, meaning light/dark). Squint in order to see the light and dark tones. For nuances in the shadows you can use a half tone, which should be closer in value to your dark. In effect, you are using three tones for this drawing, light, half-tone and dark. While you are squinting at the scene,

Right: Subtractive tone

decide which parts fall into each tonal category and try to stick to this.

Proceed by rubbing out the light shapes in the scene. The actual method of rubbing can leave expressive marks (like a woodcut, sometimes), which you may wish to honour. Make sure that you give equal attention to all parts of the picture — figure and background. Then move on to the areas that fall into the mid-tone range.

There may be occasions in this drawing when you become confused between concerns for colour and those of cast shadow. Remember that you are trying to depict the effect of light as it falls on forms within your visual field, in order to give substance and space to the scene that you are portraying. You may need to compromise in some of your descriptions of colour. If a colour is dark within the scene and there is a discernible shadow on it, you may have to describe the lit area of that colour with a half-tone and the shadow area with a dark tone. If the colour is so dark that the shadow on it is hardly discernible, use your darkest tone for the whole area of that colour.

As the drawing progresses, you may wish to play with the way in which light or dark areas run across more than one form, letting the tone consume forms. Should you wish to differentiate between two elements in the picture, you can use endotropic or exotropic shadow, or a line, to denote the edge.

PROJECT 3
ADDITIVE TONE

One 2-hour drawing
Materials: *A1 cartridge paper, charcoal or black pastel, hard eraser*
The approach in this project is to begin by establishing broad areas of tonal value, and then work into them to differentiate form and volume.

Pose and illuminate the model and surroundings. Squint at the scene through half-closed eyes and determine the pattern of dark tones across the whole subject. At this stage, also determine in your mind's eye the scale and composition of your drawing.

Quickly proceed to rough in the tonal areas — do not deliberate or hesitate. It is not necessary to measure, plot or draw in the contours of the forms to bind the areas of tone together. Approach the drawing with a relaxed and intuitive approximation of the scale of the tonal areas. This part of the drawing should take you about 20 minutes.

Smudge your drawing with newsprint so that you have dark and mid-tones over the entire paper. There are a number of reasons for doing this. Firstly, it will push the dark tones back, so that they do not look like the last marks made on the paper. If they are not knocked back, they are likely to sit in front of the picture plane and fight against the illusion you are trying to create. In other words, they will read as deposits of dark pigment on the paper instead of shadows in space. Secondly, a mid-tone ground is created into which you can work highlights and on which you can re-establish the darker tones. Thirdly, it should make you less precious about reassessing and reworking your drawing. A drawing is seldom, if ever, right until it is finished.

Over the top of the smudged drawing, re-find the scene in front of you with a line. This can be a gestural line, a continuous line, or vectors of analysis (for those who wish to be more deliberate).

Reassess and readdress the tonal balance. Use your eraser to create the light areas, and consider emphasising or redrawing some of the darker ones.

As with the previous drawing, consider using endotropic and exotropic shadows or highlights — with discretion — to distinguish the different features.

The line can be left as it is, or added to in order to describe parts of the scene in more detail. In either case, use the line advisedly. If you put outlines around all the features in the scene, objects will look like cardboard cut-outs and the drawing will have no atmosphere. Let light or shadow break across the line, creating a drawing of atmosphere and light.

> Remember that the first stag
> of this drawing is an approxi-
> mation. As you develop the
> drawing, do not try to force
> what you are looking at to
> conform absolutely to what yo
> put down to begin with.
> If you are consistent in your
> treatment of the different
> features in the scene, you
> should achieve a strong evoca
> tion of the incidence and effec
> of the light on the model and
> surroundings.

Right: Additive to

CHAPTER 4

BUILDING BLOCKS

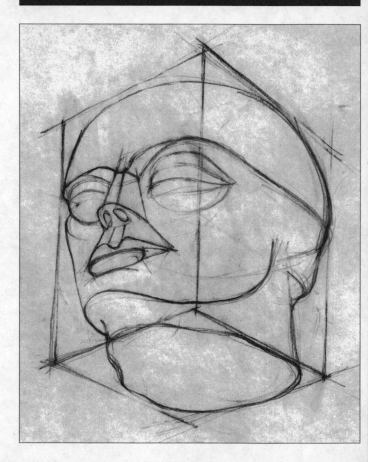

When we use the word 'form', we mean the three-dimensional object, or the illusion of it on a two-dimensional surface. By shape, we mean any two-dimensional area – and only that. Shape is flat; it does not possess the third dimension – depth. This distinction may seem pedantic, but it is very important because the two are quite different.

From an early age children develop an ability to perceive and manage shapes and forms in order to understand and use the things that are around them. They are given games that test and develop their awareness of form and shape. Two such games are particularly illuminating for the artist.

The puzzle that involves matching differently formed blocks into matching slots develops a child's awareness of shapes. This aptitude is crucial for representing and understanding the objective world. In 'Through the Window' we touched briefly on one system – peephole perspective – for projecting a form onto a two-dimensional surface and there are several other possibilities.

Shape

Suffice it to say that much of drawing can be understood as a projection from a three-dimensional space onto a two-dimensional surface.

The second toy that reflects on the theme of this chapter is the building block. Children encounter and use the blocks in different

Form

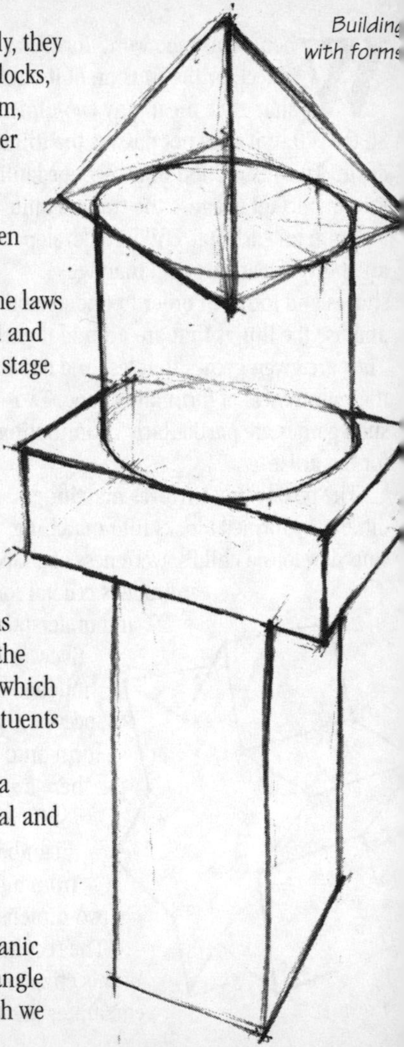

ways at different stages. Initially, they explore the physicality of the blocks, picking them up, dropping them, biting them, hitting two together and so on. In this way, they assay and test their bodies and senses with the blocks. They then begin to organise the blocks in various ways, learning about the laws and forces in the natural world and about their own dexterity. This stage is characterised by the tower, which a child will build up and then cause to topple.

In the final stage, children are intent on building models of objects — trains, tractors, castles, people and so on — based on their own observations and imaginations. They build the complex forms of the world in which they live with the simple constituents of a set of blocks, reducing the complexity of a steam train to a combination of a few cylindrical and rectangular forms.

FUNDAMENTAL SHAPES
There are three prime or inorganic shapes — the rectangle, the triangle and the ellipse — through which we

Building
with forms

48

can understand the infinite number of organic possibilities. We can use these shapes to analyse and assess more complex shapes, and the relationships between shapes, in order to assemble more elaborate figures. In these instances, what we are analysing is the flat figure, or the figure rendered flat.

FUNDAMENTAL FORMS

To understand three-dimensional objects we use form – actual form or the illusion of form. There are three categories of fundamental form: the rectangular, including the cube; the ovoid, including the sphere; and the cone and its section, including the cylinder. We can use these forms in drawing to 'crate', or package, the complex forms that we see around us. Alternatively, we can recreate the complexities of the figure by using the forms as building blocks.

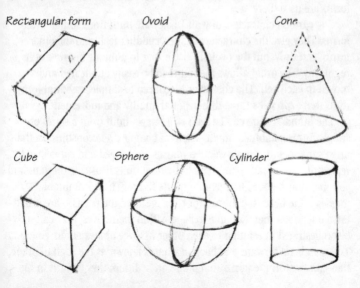

Rectangular form   Ovoid   Cone

Cube   Sphere   Cylinder

To 'crate' the world, we use the rectangular form more often than the other two. Its relationships are constant, being built around the straight line and the right angle, and measurements are therefore easier to take. However, we can use any of the fundamental forms to assemble objects in our vision, depending on the drawing's context and purpose.

In sculpture, different cultures have restricted themselves mainly to just one of the three categories. The sculptures of the East are characterised by the use of the cone in describing the body. The head may still conform to the ovoid, but the rest of the figure is a series of cylinders. In the Occidental tradition, which emerged in Ancient Greece and reached its nadir in the Italian Renaissance, the ovoid and sphere were used as standard building blocks. The cube is used mainly in Africa. And although some African masks and sculptures are built with cubes and rectangular blocks and planes, quite a wide range of fundamental forms are used there.

The cartoon characters of Walt Disney are built from simple ovoid forms. They give the characters a cuter, cuddlier feel than the other forms, certainly; but the ovoid is also easier to animate because of its regularity. The ovoid allows the figure to be easily duplicated and moved in each cell. The character is reduced to simple, essential form-units that express its three-dimensional quality and movement.

The human figure can be seen as a puppet built from a series of simple forms combined into a system of complex relationships. In the artist's mannekin, simple wooden masses are hinged and connected to represent the human figure. The individual units illustrate the standard volumes that we need to attend to in the figure. Three immutable masses – the head, the thorax (or rib-cage) and the pelvis – are articulated one to another. Not able to bend within themselves, they can only be orchestrated in relation to each other in three planes of movement. They can bend forward and back in what is known as the sagitall plane; they can twist in the horizontal plane; in addition, they can tilt in the transverse plane. The hinges connecting each mass to the next – the neck and the abdomen – compress and stretch to accommodate the movement of the head, thorax and pelvis.

We can consider further volumes of the figure organised along the main bones – the upper and lower arms and the upper and lower legs. These, too, cannot bend or twist within their masses, but only in relation to each other. The hands and feet can each be considered an individual unit of form initially, but they can also be drawn by building them up from the individual units forming fingers and toes. Although the head can be considered as a single, discrete form, it is in fact comprised of two interconnected forms – the mandible, or jawbone, and the cranium, or skull. Particularly when the head is seen sideways on, it is important that these two forms are noted and represented.

PROJECT 1

THE FIGURE AS A 'BLOCK PUPPET'

Two 15-minute drawings
Materials: *A1 cartridge paper, charcoal or conté chalk*
Begin each drawing with a light mapping of the figure (gestural, continuous line, or vectors of analysis). Keep the drawing light but confident, as you are going to superimpose the second stage on top of the initial mapping.

Imagine you have only simple blocks based on the cube and rectangular form with which to construct the figure. On top of the initial mapping, place these blocks and sections to represent the figure in front of you (illustrated overleaf). You can use a wedge for the feet, for example, as this is a section of a rectangular solid. Make sure that the blocks slot into each other.

Complete two drawings from two different angles.

Use a unique block for each section of the figure: head, thorax, pelvis, upper arms, lower arms, upper legs, lower legs, feet, hands, neck and abdomen.

The figure built from blocks based on the rectangular form and the cube

THE FIGURE AS A PUPPET BUILT FROM CYLINDERS

Two 15-minute drawings
Materials: *A1 cartridge paper,
charcoal or conté chalk
The figure is built up using cylindrical
units of the correct proportions.*

Proceed as in the previous
project, but using cylinders
instead of blocks. The head looks
peculiar as a cylinder, and is best
considered as an ovoid form for
this exercise.

The figure built from cylinders

THE OVOID FIGURE

Two 15-minute drawings
Materials: *A1 cartridge paper, conté or soft pencil, or biro
For the ovoid figure, use the continuous line (see 'Hand, Eye and Mind', Project 5). The
line should swing around, describing interlocking ellipses that also represent the
interlocking ovoid forms.*

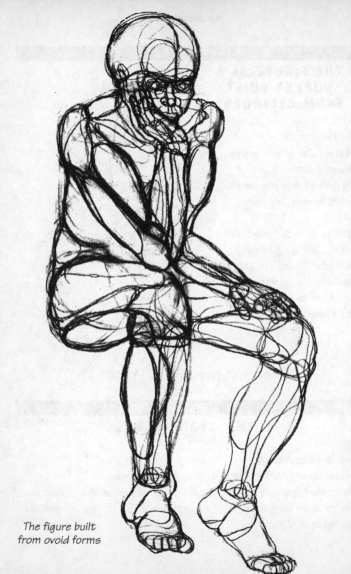

*The figure built
from ovoid forms*

Do two drawings, spending 15 minutes on each. Look for the major masses of the head, thorax and pelvis, and also make a preliminary attempt to describe muscle, fat, sinew and bone with the ellipse.

Postural analysis and form

PROJECT 4

POSTURAL ANALYSIS AND FORM

Three 15-minute drawings
Materials: *A1 cartridge paper, conté or soft pencil*

This exercise is best realised if the model is standing upright, not foreshortened in any way.
Lightly place the figure with a gestural or continuous line drawing. Over this initial drawing, draw and assess the masses of head, thorax and pelvis by 'crating' them. Assess the posture of the figure by determining the angles of the long arm and leg bones (see 'Through the Window', Methods of analysis) and the angles of the rectangles that can be formed around the three main masses. The lines formed across the base of the chin, the brow

and the top of the head should be parallel. The shoulders form the top of the thorax; a line drawn from shoulder to shoulder should be parallel to the lower edge of the rib-cage. The top of the pelvis is gained by drawing a vector between the two bones of the iliac crest, the two pieces of bone at the front, around the top bikini line. The bottom of the pelvic box is at the groin. Determine the axes through these boxes.

PROJECT 5
THE PLANAL FIGURE

One 4-hour drawing
Materials: *A1 cartridge paper, soft or conté pencil*
The figure is analysed in terms of a continuous series of changing planes.

Use vectors of analysis (see 'Through the Window', Project 1) to map out the figure. Draw the figure at a size that completely fills the paper, as it is mass, not space, that you are predominantly concerned with in this project. Determine the posture of the figure and lightly mark these accents and angles on the drawing.

Consider what the masses of the figure would look like 'crated'. Lightly mark in the side and front planes of the crates. Then, starting at the point where two forms meet, show the movement around each form as a series of planes. Use these planes, or plates, to represent other complex forms in the figure. Proceed until you have described the whole figure in three dimensions as a progression of planes.

The planal figure

CHAPTER 5

INSIDE OUT, OUTSIDE IN

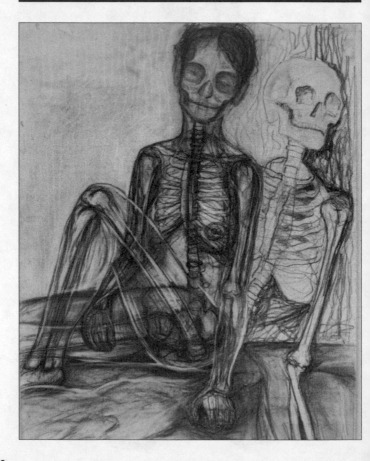

Kimon Nicolaides advises that: 'Anatomy in the hands of the artist is merely another instrument for making the figure articulate and clear. It is never to be thought of as an end in itself. Only a means to an end.'

The figure is a complete entity and needs to be considered as such. It is nigh on impossible to distinguish between muscle, bone, fat and flesh in the life figure in the way that anatomy books are wont to do. The particularities of the individual model and the poses he or she takes up will always create unique situations, and you will need to use a good deal of detective work and invention to equate the information in an anatomy book with your own observations of the model.

The sculptors of Classical Greece, whose proclaimed aim was naturalism, continuously re-invented the anatomy of their figure sculptures. Michelangelo, Raphael and other Renaissance artists likewise created their own musculature for their figures. In comic strips featuring the superheroes of today, anatomy is distorted and exaggerated to create a supra-real musculature. Ovoid form is laid over ovoid to create bulging supermen and women. We need to invent and deploy some metaphor, beyond what we see, in all drawing if it is to carry our observations and thoughts about the figure and its anatomy.

An understanding and knowledge of anatomy is useful in the representation of the human figure. It will, however, take a great deal of study and drawing (the two are not independent activities in this instance) to reconcile and use knowledge of anatomy to enrich observed phenomena. This chapter is a first step, laying the basis for a reconciliation between observation and knowledge by looking at what can be ascertained from the outside, and building our knowledge of the figure on the inside.

FROM THE OUTSIDE IN

Imagine a few oranges placed on a table-top. One could draw them in a number of ways: concentrating on their silhouette, their texture, their form, or how they are lit, for example. If you were to throw a linen sheet over the table-top and oranges, covering the oranges and table-top in a continuous layer, you would still see that there were orange-like forms under the sheet. Ways of drawing this set-up would be less obvious, although one way might be to draw the forms of the oranges and then progress to the sheet.

Oranges on a table

If a number of oranges were piled up on the table-top and covered with a sheet, all you would know was that there was a large mound under the sheet. Only the oranges on the outside of the stack, those that come into contact with the sheet, would be individually discernible. To draw this set-up you would need to start by thinking of the mound as a form in its own right (regardless of its constituent elements), and then address the individual orange forms (spheres) that press through the sheet.

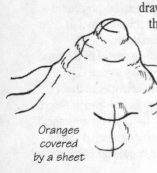

Oranges covered by a sheet

Perhaps you can see where this is leading with regard to the human figure. The body can be thought of as a number of major forms – upper arms, lower arms, thorax, abdomen and so on – each made up of minor forms – muscle, bone, sinew and tendon – covered by the dermatic membrane. This is composed of cutaneous tissue, the skin, and subcutaneous tissue, the layer of fat beneath it. The weight and substance of the dermatic membrane, and whether it is tightly or loosely drawn over the forms, are additional factors that you need to think about when drawing the figure. Also, the dermatic membrane varies from person to person. In the case of a body-builder, the subcutaneous tissue is reduced to a minimum and the skin is drawn taut over the body, attached in all places to the muscle forms beneath and therefore revealing the 'cut' of each muscle. For the rest of us, our fleshy exterior has thickness and weight. In places it is taut and attached to the muscle beneath and in other places it is slack and loose.

Muscles, bones and sinews can be seen as a series of forms beneath the skin.

PROJECT 1
FROM THE OUTSIDE IN

One 3-hour drawing
Materials: *A1 cartridge paper (black or white), pastel, conté or chalk (white or black can be used)*
This project addresses the forms of the human anatomy that can be observed at and through the dermatic membrane, in order to represent them through the way in which they come into contact with this membrane.

The drawing is built in two stages. Consider the human figure in the same way that you did the covered oranges on the table, that is, as a series of forms covered by a membrane. In the first stage of the drawing, try to divine the major and minor forms of the figure's anatomy from your observations and record them as a drawing. The aim in the second stage is to describe and use the surface covering the forms to qualify the relative positions of the forms and establish their three-dimensional nature. The first part of the drawing should take two-thirds of the total time.

Stage 1

Pose the model so that you have a good view of most of the figure. On a fairly large scale, quickly and lightly map the figure, seeking generalised proportions and posture, using the fundamental forms as they apply to the basic units of the human body (see 'Building Blocks') as your elementary architecture. Onto these forms, you are going to graft your observations and understanding of muscle, bone and various tissues. Although you can use other forms to describe the musculature, the ovoid is the preferred unit. Renaissance artists such as Michelangelo have thought of the human figure as a gathering of ovoidal forms organised under a sculptural skin — ovoids overlapping and slotting into each other, built up on the architecture of the skeleton.

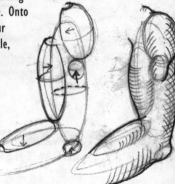

The ovoid is best for describing the musculature

As with the oranges covered with a cloth, clues to the internal form and structure of the human body are provided at the points where they interact and mould its surface covering. Something causes a contour to bulge in a

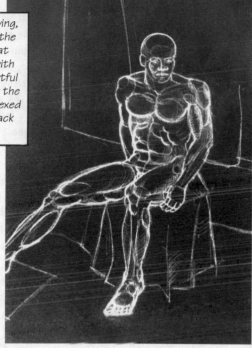

To progress the drawing, try to describe with the ovoid the forms that come into contact with the skin. If you are artful enough, you can show the hardness of bone, a flexed or flaccid muscle, slack skin and fat.

certain way, a shadow to be cast, an indentation to be made, a hollow to exist, and in this drawing you should be focusing on the causes of these effects. The effects themselves are only clues. For example, a hollow exists in a drawing only as that which is caused by two or more forms. In other words, to draw a depression you need to draw the cause of the depression, not the depression itself. This is so obvious, yet time and again students will not acknowledge that the hollow is only a feature of two forms.

Once you have constructed the major forms of the body, lightly and gesturally begin to rough in the forms you can detect under the flesh using overlapping ellipses (the silhouette of the ovoid). Make sure that the forms inform the silhouette and contours of the figure and are not compromised by a predetermined outline.

The figure is composed of ovoidal units that slot into and lie on top of each other. When beginners to drawing use the ellipse they draw it as a shape, fitting one ellipse up against another, instead of overlapping them. This will flatten the forms in the drawing. Also, the internal forms of the figure are built on different scales and in different orientations to the major forms. Avoid building the figure through only one axis and orientation, and with one scale, otherwise a 'Michelin' man — a series of ballooned forms stacked one on another — will appear. Throughout this exercise you are involved with form, not tone; try to deduce the forms under the surface.

Once you have drawn the ellipses, move to the contour, using it to define the edges of the form and to show where one form is in front of another. Use a heavier line for this. If you totally enclose a muscle form, it will flatten and read as distinct from the rest of the figure. You need to keep the forms open so that in the flow between forms you can imply skin through a continuity of surface.

Stage 2

Although the contour will have helped in creating the look of three dimensions, by using a mark that moves across the surface you can further enhance the form and see how the skin is laid over the muscle and bone.

This description of the surface of the form is evolved from an understanding of the form's cross-section. Imagine slicing a loaf of bread. The slices reveal the loaf's cross-section. The cuts are made parallel to each other on a horizontal axis, and the loaf becomes misshapen if the slices are not cut in

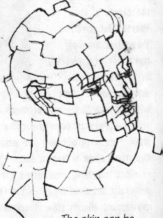

The skin can be described by the way it follows the forms.

this way. In a drawing, your analysis must be made in the plane that is either horizontal or perpendicular to the major form. You can transfer from the horizontal to the vertical plane. Henry Moore (1898-1987) used this assessment of form in his drawings.

Progress your drawing by this analysis, describing the surfaces of the ovoids and the skin stretched over them. This will develop your understanding of these forms and the way in which they modulate the surface of the body.

There are other ways of elaborating on this description of the human anatomy. For example, you can use tone to model the figure. Light each ovoid form centrally (see 'A Progession of Tone') and let tone slide and run across the forms on the surface of the figure like a continuous ripple.

You can also combine cross-sectional analysis with tonal modulations, developing the tone with crosshatching built up of lines that take their directions from the surface of the form. This is sometimes referred to as 'bracelet shading'. The bracelet encompasses the form and also sits on the horizontal plane. Examine Michelangelo's drawings to see wonderful examples of both.

FROM THE INSIDE OUT

Human anatomy is complex. Bones are not regular; ligaments squeeze and pull in all directions at the meeting point of two bones; muscles and tendons run in all directions, wrapping through and over each other as they connect to the bone. And on top of all this, there is flesh. Yet, in spite of this complexity, human anatomy is based on the simple logic of balance and motion. Human form is governed by and fashioned to accommodate the laws of mechanics and dynamics; we are built the way we are because of the activities that we perform in our everyday lives.

Gravity acts on the human frame. Our limbs, head, thorax and pelvis are articulated one to another in a way that allows both for our movements and for the effects of gravity. In motion and at rest, one part of the body will move to compensate for the shift in weight caused by the movement or position of another part.

The bones can be regarded as the structural members in our dynamic human architecture. Ligaments are the springs that bind the bones together. The muscles are the motivators, pushing and pulling one bone in relation to another in order to create movement. Where muscles connect to the skeleton, they flatten out and attach like so many rubber bands. These connections are the tendons or sinews. Muscles express the law of motion, 'for every action there is an equal and opposite reaction', and are therefore paired. If one muscle pulls two bones open, another must be able to draw them closed.

Muscles are scaled appropriately to the length and mass of the units they need to

The human skeleton and musculature

> *With all the drawings, try to evolve an understanding of what the muscles act on — what mechanisms they activate. Look for the muscles that are tensed in particular actions and poses. If you include this type of information in your drawings, you will find that anatomy is transformed from the dryly diagrammatic into the life of a drawing,*

move. For instance, the muscle that attaches a limb to the main skeletal frame is larger than those that move the digits at the end of the limb. Popeye is a freak, possessing forearms that are disproportionately larger than his atrophied upper arm – excusable in a cartoon character but not in an anatomically accurate depiction of the human figure.

To understand anatomy really well, you need knowledge of how the body moves, and you need to be able to place what you observe or learn about the figure within the framework of this movement.

PROJECT 2
FROM THE INSIDE OUT

One 5-hour drawing
Materials: *A1 or double A1 cartridge paper, conté or soft pencil*

If you are feeling bold you can use double A1 paper for this drawing, otherwise stick to A1 cartridge. You will need reference material on both the skeleton and the musculature. A real skeleton would be convenient if you have access to one. Otherwise, use an anatomical chart, anatomy books or a model skeleton. The anatomical charts found in gyms are useful as they explain which muscles are used for different movements.

Ask the model to assume the same pose as in Project I. (If you want to save on model fees, or are not able to secure a model, you can transcribe the contours of the figure from your drawing for Project I.) If you have a skeleton, position it next to the model and in the same position.

Begin by plotting the model on your paper, analysing posture and proportion. Then, using your reference material, draw the skeleton within the contours of the figure, assessing the positions of different parts of the skeleton by observing the points where bones come into contact with the skin. On top of this drawing develop the musculature, using observation and

common sense to organise the
muscles as they come into play
in this pose. However, it would
be a shame to bury the skeleton
completely, so try to leave some
of the skeleton visible.
You could also draw some of
the flesh in places.

   Throughout the evolution
of this drawing you

should constantly
compare your findings with those
in the previous project. They are,
after all, two different approaches
to the one problem and by
comparing the aspects of anatomy
that you can observe with those

Drawing from the inside out

that you can reference, you can attack the subject on two fronts. You can
develop this approach further by doing paired drawings of details of the
figure, learning and applying the muscle names as you work. You can also
repeat the exercise for different poses. This bringing together of what you
know and can learn with what you can discover through seeing, provides a
good introduction not only to anatomy but to other enquiries as well.

CHAPTER 6

MARKING TIME

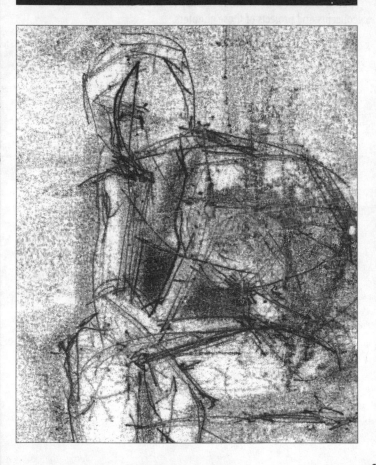

In the previous chapters we have concentrated exclusively on space and form and their representation. We ignored all indicators of time in order to create a situation in which all relationships were spatial and constant. It was necessary to do so in order to clarify the concepts and projects of those chapters.

An experience is, however, shaped in both space and time. An image without time is therefore impossible, although we may contrive the illusion of it in order to match the finite, static condition of a drawing. The 'instant point' (a moment without time) may be used as an aesthetic notion, but in reality a fraction of time bounds any experience, no matter how small (for example, the time of many photographs is about 1/60 of a second).

If drawings really are to be life drawings, rather than merely drawings of a figure, you need to discover how time can be contained in them. This can be addressed in terms of either the image itself (movement and expression), or the action of drawing (action and expression).

SINGLE IMAGES

With the aid of an electronic motor-wind, the professional photographer can fire away a number of shots of an action, and then selects the frame that captures the action in the most dramatic way. In the same way, the artist can select the moment in a sequence of actions that best conveys the whole movement – the *exemplary image*.

Alternatively, the artist can distil the whole sequence into one image, taking features from each of the instant images that a camera may record, placing and integrating them into a single image to give a synopsis of the sequence – the *synoptic image*.

MOVEMENT

Movement and expression can also be conveyed through the deviant and the unstable. We establish and can recognise positions of rest and normality. We can tell whether a body in a particular position can remain balanced. If balance is not established, we feel the body to be in motion – anticipating the sequence of movements needed to propel the body and overcome the pull of gravity. The ground anchors the body, so the figure's relationship to the ground also gives clues to its movement.

In movement, and especially extreme movement – form appears to dissolve. Obviously it is difficult to establish the boundaries of a form when it is in motion, as we rely on fixing its edge in a fixed space. Therefore, the broken or erased outline can be used as an indicator of movement. Multiple outlines, or the gestural outline, can also be used to indicate the moving figure.

A stable structure

An unstable structure

71

Emotion can be recognised in deviations from a neutral expression.

EXPRESSION

If the face at rest is taken as normal, or neutral, then an emotion can be expressed, and recognised, through any deviation from this. Our own recognition or memory of a situation or context will also facilitate our reading of the events or emotions being depicted. Some artists have codified and exaggerated movements of the body and face in order to create heightened emotion. Such emotion is melodramatic, appearing as the acting out of a feeling rather than the result of a feeling.

MULTIPLE IMAGES

An image or narrative can be portrayed as a collection of 'instants', either by depicting images at regular intervals during the action, thereby creating a sequence of actions, or by darting in and out of the sequence, picking out moments from which the course of events can be unravelled. In either case, the spacing of the images at regular intervals in time is understood by the viewer, who can reconstruct the event in order to evoke the movement.

To break up a movement into a sequence of actions, you can divide the drawing into discrete cells of action, like a story-board or comic strip, or you can use the space and objects in the setting surrounding the model to divide the drawing into units of activity.

Various acts within an action or event can be included in a drawing without thought for their chronological order, or different views or moments in the action can be combined or overlapped to create a unified action.

PROJECT 1
THE EXEMPLARY IMAGE

One 30-minute drawing
Materials: *A1 cartridge paper, charcoal or black pastel, or conté stick or charcoal pencil*

Ask the model to enact a simple action, such as rising off a seat, putting on clothes, or waking up. Then ask her to hold the action at a particularly dramatic moment.

Draw — with an appropriate drawing language — for 30 minutes, concentrating on the pose as an instant in the complete action.

> *The environment is less important with a small movement because moving forms are contrasted with still forms, whereas when the whole body moves the moving form must be calibrated against a static space.*

This can be repeated for an expression of emotion, such as surprise or horror, which you can consider as either an action of the whole body or just of the face.

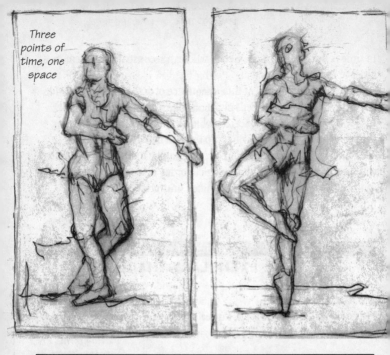

Three points of time, one space

PROJECT 2

FIVE POINTS OF TIME, ONE SPACE

One 2½-hour drawing
Materials: *A1 cartridge paper, charcoal or black pastel*

You are going to draw five selected, separate moments in the movement against a constant environment. Ask the model to move and select five points at which you want the model to freeze. Make sure that all five points of the movement fit into one view. Use line or continuous line for this project. Draw the figure at the start of the sequence together with the surroundings, taking about half an hour. Then proceed to the second

position. Draw this in the correct scale and position in space in relation to the first stage of the drawing. If this pose overlaps the first, you can erase part or all of the previous drawing, leaving just its faint impression.

Continue in the same way for the other chosen moments, keeping to the same scale and within the same space. This drawing also becomes an exercise in measurement and proportion. If the model moves a long way between each position, and there isn't much overlapping, you can repeat the exercise with smaller movements. If the model sneezes, for instance, some of her/him will be still while other parts move.

PROJECT 3

FIVE CELLS OF ACTION

Five 20-minute drawings
Materials: *A1 cartridge paper, charcoal or black pastel, or conté stick, or charcoal pencil*

In this project you are going to make a sequence of drawings of the action. Ask the model to make an action (it can be the same as in Project 2). Stop the action at five moments, making a separate drawing of each. Again use line or continuous line. On this occasion the environment is not important, but the figure needs to maintain a constant scale.

Five cells of action

PROJECT 4

THE SIMULTANEOUS IMAGE

One 4-hour drawing
Materials: *A1 cartridge paper, black pastel or charcoal*

In this drawing you will move around the still subject, gathering up different views, and present them as one image. Draw with a line.

Over 3 hours take up five different viewpoints and draw from them. The scale of the figure may be very different in each view. Draw the entire view in all five stations, overlapping one view over another. Once you have completed all five views, activate the drawing with tone. Use exotropic or

> If the image becomes very complex or confusing, you can erase parts of the previous view.

endotropic shadow (see 'A Progression of Tone') to pick out the edges of forms and also to develop abstract rhythms over the surface of the drawing. You can fill in the shapes left by overlapping views to clarify the image or to develop it aesthetically. This last part should take an hour.

THE ACTION OF DRAWING

We have considered the moving subject and some possibilities for its depiction. We can also move in relation to the subject, taking different views of the scene and drawing these. However, life, or its expression, can also be reflected in our own perceptual activity and the temporal aspects of our drawing action. The way in which we negotiate a drawing, apart from what we are representing, can reflect our attitude to and understanding of our world. The early marks that are the scaffolding on which the final drawing is built can be left in evidence in the finished work. Like an archaeologist, the viewer can read in these buried marks a trail of the artist's endeavours, thoughts and feelings.

NAVIGATING A DRAWING

One 3-hour drawing
Materials: *A1 cartridge paper, charcoal, eraser*

This drawing is made through a series of alternating decisions and revisions. Draw the model on a scale that more or less fills the paper.

Make the drawing with a constantly moving hand — a scansion — moving the drawing tool into contact with the paper and then lifting it off, leaving a broken trail of marks that follow the scanning eye as it fixes and then breaks from its subject, only to pick it up again at another spot.

The marks are made with certainty and then questioned (at this point the hand moves away from the paper). At a particular point (about 20 minutes into the drawing), rub the drawing back with a hand, cloth or piece of paper, leaving a smudged base on which to build new decisions. Work over the top of the first drawing with the same broken scansion, but now introduce an eraser — not as a tool of correction but to work in highlights as drawing actions. These need not conform to a directional light, but can abstract tonal rhythms for the sake of the drawing itself.

Carry on building up the drawing and breaking it down until it is complete. Earlier decisions will lie under later marks, creating an abstract space where the last actions are suspended in front of earlier ones. This allows the viewer to read in the drawing the time spent thinking and doing, and draws them into the act of drawing itself.

Right: Navigating a drawing

CONCLUSION

Leonardo da Vinci wrote in his notebooks: 'Life is long. In rivers, the water that you touch is the last of what has passed and the first of that which comes, so with time present.' A drawing dips into this river, picking out an aesthetic present that is part of the coursing stream. In order to know the stream, you must touch it. But not only do you touch the stream; it touches back. It is important to reflect in your drawings on the intertwining of yourself and your world.

Merleau Ponty wrote: 'Before the essence as before the fact, all we must do is situate ourselves within the being we are dealing with instead of dealing with it from the outside – or, what amounts to the same thing, what we have to do is put it back into the fabric of our lives.' (*The Visible and the Invisible*). To place what we draw into 'the fabric of our lives' is an imperative for life drawing. You cannot be uninvolved, and in your involvement lies the seed of your drawing.

We have covered a great deal in the small space of this book, but there is still much that lies beyond. We have dealt predominantly with the representation of the figure and environment in a perspective space, but there are other spatial systems. Some quite amazing drawings of the figure have been made using schematic or diagrammatic approaches. Projections other than perspectival ones can also be used in representing a human being in the world, as evidenced in many great works from the East. All of this remains to be explored or used, as and when necessary, to develop representations of your own observations and opinions, actions and stories, thoughts and feelings.

Published by Arcturus Publishing Limited
For Bookmart Limited
Registered Number 2372865
Trading as Bookmart Limited
Desford Road
Enderby
Leicester
LE9 5AD

This edition published 1996

Printed and bound in Great Britain

© Arcturus Publishing Limited/P. Stanyer, T. Rosenberg

ISBN 1 900032 90 2

Text: Terry Rosenberg
With thanks to my wife Pernilla and daughter Tassia for
all their love and support.

Editor: Helen Douglas-Cooper
Design: Wilson Design Associates

ACKNOWLEDGEMENTS
The authors and publishers would like to thank the
following for lending drawings for reproduction:
Francesca Cesati, Miriam Freitag, Elaine French, Robert
Grose, Sue Kennington, Lisa Meaney, Jenny Scott,
Josephine Shepherd David Todd, Marco Toro, Debbie
True; and thanks to all the students who lent drawings
for possible inclusion. Additional drawings by Peter
Stanyer and Terry Rosenberg. Rembrandt etching repro-
duced by permission of the Rijksmuseum, Amsterdam.

The authors would like to thank the City Literary
Institute and the Chelsea School of Art and Design,
where they teach many of these drawing programmes.